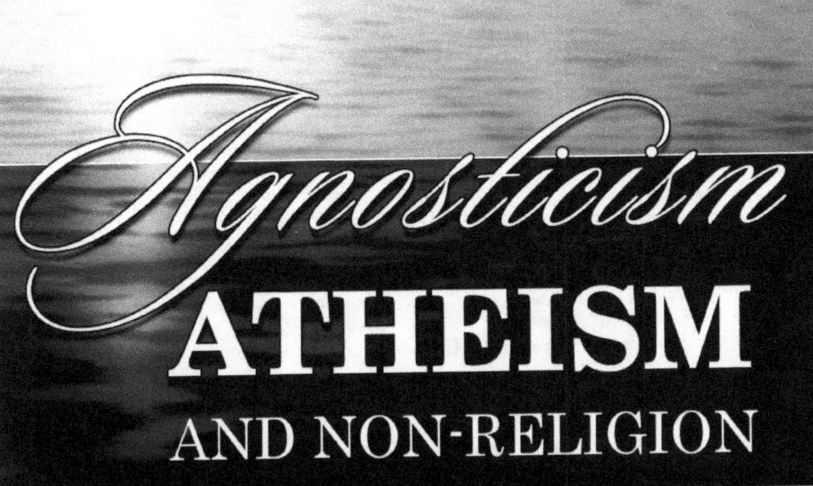

Agnosticism ATHEISM AND NON-RELIGION

By Oracle Claretta Pam

Agnosticism, Atheism and Non-Religion

Oracle Claretta Pam

Oracle Claretta Pam

Published and printed in the United States by Sacred Vision Press, an imprint of Innovative Publishers, Inc., a division of Global Nebula, LLC, Boston, Massachusetts.

Agnosticism, Atheism and Non-Religion

Library of Congress Control Number: 2013944032

ISBN-10: 1-4913-1620-9	ISBN-13: 978-1-4913-1620-7 Paperback
ISBN-10: 1-4913-1621-7	ISBN-13: 978-1-4913-1621-4 Hardback
ISBN-10: 1-4913-1622-5	ISBN-13: 978-1-4913-1622-1 Kindle
ISBN-10: 1-4913-1623-3	ISBN-13: 978-1-4913-1623-8 iBook
ISBN-10: 1-4913-1624-1	ISBN-13: 978-1-4913-1624-5 Nook
ISBN-10: 1-4913-1625-X	ISBN-13: 978-1-4913-1625-2 Audiobook

Published and printed in the United States by
Innovative Publishers, Inc., Boston, Massachusetts

10 9 8 7 6 5 4 3 2 1 14 15 16 17 18

An interpretation of the printing code: is the number of the books printing. The rightmost number of the second series of numbers is the year of the books printing. For example, a printing code of 1–14 shows that the first printing occurred in 2014.

First edition. August 2014

DEDICATION

To everyone and everything in this universe.

Most sacred vision books are available at special quantity discounts for bulk purchases first sales promotions, premiums, fundraising, or educational use. Special books, or book excerpts, can be created to fit specific needs. For details, email info@innovative-publishers.com.

Upcoming titles:

Bahai Faith
Buddhism
Cao Dai
Catholicism
Christianity
Confucianism
Hinduism
Humanism
Islam
Jainism
Jehovas Witnesses
Juche North Korea
Kabbalah
Judaism
Natural Law
Neopaganism
New Age
Primal Faith
Primal Indigenous
Rastafarianism
Scientology
Shinto
Sikhism
Spiritism
Taoism
Tarahumara Beliefs
Tenrikyo
The Occult
African Traditional - Diasporic
Unificationism
Unitarian Universalism
Zoroastrianism

Agnosticism, Atheism and Non-Religion

CONTENTS

ACKNOWLEDGMENTS

A special note of thanks to the congregation at the Universal Life Church Monastery of Massachusetts both online and on the ground. Your encouragement and participation and spreading the understanding of all belief systems is what will effect positive change in this world and beyond.

I

INTRODUCTION

It is interesting to consider how often people make unverified claims when discussing the subject of religion. Rather than simply exploring the presence or absence of God, their focus remains perpetually fixed on trying to prove or disprove mere speculations, which in turn limits them from discovering further possibilities. In doing so, religion is irredeemably politicized in the public and private spheres of human life, allowing for deliberate distortion and dogma. At the same time, however, to separate religion from personal bias would be to distance oneself from a supposed God for the purpose of objective examination. This unyielding gap between Man and the Unknown is often problematic as it ends up blurring the reality of 'what is', while subjective experience attempts to eliminate this distance entirely

– though by any means necessary.

Consequently, this gap has a massive influence on people's perception of an all-encompassing, immaculate Creator. While some refer to Holy Scriptures as the sacred word of God, others reject it outright, claiming evidence that points to the contrary. In addition, there are also those who maintain a somewhat flexible stance, believing that perhaps the only thing one can be certain of is one's uncertainty. Over the years, however, scientists and philosophers have gone beyond metaphysical assumptions concerning the true nature of God, and have instead attempted to logically confirm His existence or non-existence altogether. This is becoming an increasingly important part of, indeed, any religion today as people continue to seek nothing but the absolute truth.

In this case, we must clarify what we mean by the term "religion" before we attempt to define atheism and agnosticism. If we are to assume that religion simply means being devoted to a supreme force that controls the state of the Universe (taking away any and all supernatural elements from the equation), then essentially each of us have a religion. A young girl might strongly believe in Jesus as her ultimate savior, and that he died for the sins of humanity – in which case, it is clearly Jesus who defines her religion.

Likewise, if others deny God, but are as devoted to accumulating wealth as the young girl is to Jesus, then indeed they too have a religion; only, it is money that they worship in the given context. As seen from this example, several complications arise in deciding upon a universally acceptable definition of "religion" as everyone holds a different opinion as to who or what God could possibly be. Of course, if we are to interpret religion as a belief in an omnipotent Creator, the Knower of all things, who breathed life into this Universe, created the heavens and the earth, giving purpose and meaning to everything within and beyond our lives, then perhaps it can be said that not everyone believes in such a God – though they may inadvertently replace Him with their personal idols (whoever or whatever they may be).

As such, the question of God's existence cannot be answered simply by presenting favorable or unfavorable evidence, for there are other equally relevant concerns that stem from the debate henceforth. Granted, for a moment, that there is a God – how are we to prove His oneness as described in Abrahamic faith? Similarly, how would we prove the multiplicity of gods? Indeed many have attempted to answer these questions, citing the perfect laws of Nature as their justification. Such perfection, according to monotheists, clearly points toward the existence of a singular deity. The logic behind this argument seems to suggest that multiplicity results in conflict and, thus, manifests as an imbalance within the cosmic order. Unfortunately, this may not be very convincing to followers of polytheistic religions, who attribute the same Natural perfection to a number of gods and goddesses.

Even more perplexing is the fact that some of the greatest philosophers in history described the laws of Nature as an aftermath of the Big Bang and, thus, a confirmation that there is no God – single or multiple. This is a fundamental difference between theists and atheists, in that, atheists reject any and all notions of an all-pervading, independent entity, supernatural or not, who created and controls the Universe. They deviate from agnostics when they attempt to confirm this assumption, believing that there is conclusive evidence to justify their claim. Agnostics, however, choose to draw no absolute conclusions and remain open to both possibilities due to a lack of concrete evidence. While there are different shades within the agnostic thought, it is associated primarily with English philosopher, Thomas Henry Huxley, who coined the term to differentiate himself from Gnostics or those who claim to know the absolute truth. In addition, agnosticism is deeply embedded in the philosophy of not just skepticism, but also introspection, which explores the various possibilities concerning one's own existence. As an integral part of agnostic attitude, it is imperative to question reality at all times and suspend judgment where there is no room for possibilities other than the ones stated.

The relationship between atheism and agnosticism is a particularly close one, though many argue that the agnostic perspective is fundamentally different, even from theism. By taking the middle-ground, agnostics may often appear to be in line with, both, believers and non-believers alike. However, it can also be interpreted as having little, if anything, to do with either school of thought. This is because, for many people who strictly reject or believe in the existence of God, the evasive "I don't know" response essentially amounts to nothing. Prominent British philosopher of the 20th century, Bertrand Russell, addressed this problem by writing extensively on the overlapping of agnosticism and atheism. Identifying himself as, both, an atheist and agnostic, he explained that many seekers ultimately deduce that there is no plausible way to confirm the existence or non-existence of God, but they find it difficult to label themselves anything specific.

Regarding this particular issue, Richard Dawkins, author of the critically acclaimed book, *"The God Delusion"*, presents two situations in which agnosticism may or may not be justified. Indecision based on reason, he claims, is justified as it stems from the need to confirm a speculative hypothesis before accepting it. However, indecision which is permanently rooted in the belief that the Unknown can never truly be unraveled is, in his opinion, *"intellectual cowardice"* and, therefore, unjustified. As such, he expands the scope of agnosticism by defining, what he calls, "Temporary Agnosticism in Practice" (TAP), and "Permanent Agnosticism in Principle" (PAP).

There are also those who do not place their faith in any particular system of belief – not in God or science, nor even reason or spirituality. This is considered non-religion or irreligion, though it is worth noting that most of these people identify themselves as humanists or secularists rather than "non-religious". More often than not, non-religion is identified as a part of secularism, which also varies in definition for different people. Most commonly, however, it is broadly defined as an indifference towards the general concept of religion. What causes a discrepancy is how people choose to express this indifference – whether it is through hostility, intolerance, passivity or complete withdrawal. In many cases, skepticism, atheism and agnosticism are all recognized as a form of non-religion, though the most self-defining feature of this ideology is a complete apathy towards religion, more than anything else. It must not be forgotten, however, that the line between atheism, agnosticism and non-religion tends to be very thin, causing much debate over their nature and scope. Some who claim to be atheist might find that their beliefs are more in line with agnosticism, whole those who claim to be agnostic might discover they lean more towards atheism. Ultimately, it all comes down to the level of certainty (or the lack thereof) we hold in our particular beliefs.

2
DOES GOD EXIST?

As we delve deeper into the subject of God, we are left with an inevitable conflict between, what philosophers call, *a priori* and *posteriori* knowledge – the former relating to inherent knowledge, and the latter, experiential or empirical knowledge. Renowned philosopher and physician of the 16th century, John Locke, made significant contributions in the field of theology by giving birth to the concept of *"Tabula Rasa"*, suggesting that the mind is an empty slate on which we engrave ideas and beliefs. Accordingly, he claimed that the idea of God, too, is imprinted in our minds by society – an idea that is either rejected or embraced as we grow up trying to fully comprehend it. This is a part of *posteriori* knowledge in that it is determined by a series of experiences that completely alter one's perception of reality.

To take an example, if a girl is taught from an early age that God is an omniscient force of Creation, and she grows up witnessing people oppress each other in His name, it is very likely that, at some point, she may stand against oppression by dissociating from God entirely. In this case, it is the girl's experience that would lead to a rejection of this particular belief.

On the other hand, renowned philosopher from ancient Greece, Hippocrates "the father of Western medicine", argued that although much of our ideas and beliefs are passed on to us by society, there are some that we are inherently born with. He considered such ideas to be a part of intrinsic or *a priori* knowledge, in which he included the notion of God. While people may grow up to accept or reject God, Hippocrates believed that the idea is nevertheless engrained in our design. Throughout our lives, we explore this idea and draw our own conclusions, but since the notion of God is, in itself, innate – it bears the mark of the Creator, very much like a watchmaker's signature, so-to-speak. William Paley (1743-1805) was responsible for the inception of this theory, commonly referred to as "The Design or Teleological Argument" which draws parallels between the human eye and a watch, each designed with perfection and purpose. Just as the complexity of a watch reveals the existence of a watchmaker, the theory postulates that the complexity of Creation, too, proves the existence of a Supreme

Maker.

If we are to accept this theory, then God's intangible presence can perhaps be explained through the proposition that we are imperfect beings – thus, the concept of Absolute Perfection is naturally inconceivable to us. However, the theory falls short as it fails to address the origins of an assumed God. That is to say, if the watch was created by a watchmaker, then who created the watchmaker? How to we determine the origins of Absolute Perfection? This is a strong case in point for atheists, those who deny the existence of God, for it is ultimately void of logic and reason. As a result, they refuse to overlook such loopholes which, according to them, only reveal the irrationality of believing in groundless assumptions. Moreover, it ignores an alternative explanation for the complexity of Creation, which is the theory of evolution popularized by Charles Darwin. This is a highly damaging criticism of the "Design Argument", as the theory of evolution explains the origins of the Universe without assuming the existence of an invisible entity. In addition, atheists can justify their claims through scientific logic and empirical evidence, which is attributed to the Big Bang in place of improbable speculations. Whether or not the theory of evolution is able to fill the metaphysical void or convince anyone, the design argument nevertheless fails to address the counter or provide further justification.

Another philosophical proposition for the existence of God is the hugely contested "Cosmological Argument". Somewhat similar to the Design Argument, this theory is centered mainly on cause and effect relationships. Greek polymath, Aristotle, a student of Plato and teacher of Alexander the Great, was largely accredited for shedding light on this argument, listing four types of causalities to differentiate between the many kinds of causal connections. These are:

1. **Material cause:** This is a type of causation in which objects are composed of specific materials, in which case, the object is fundamentally caused by that specific material. There is no particular action involved in the process, and the material alone is responsible for the existence of the object; for instance, in the case of a wooden chair.

2. **Formal cause:** This pertains to the 'form' or arrangement of an object – a blueprint, so-to-speak, which provides an entire baseline for the object. Here, the causal connection is derived from the philosophy that *"the whole is a sum or cause of its parts"*. Accordingly, the object exists because of a simple intrinsic idea which is eventually embodied through matter. Due to this, the formal cause is also commonly referred to as the whole-part causation.

3. **Efficient cause:** The causation here is established through, what is known as, "a primary source" which effectively results in instant motion. As such, an efficient cause is mostly exemplified through one domino falling over another, setting off an immediate reaction in the form of causal movement.

4. **Final cause:** Also referred to as *'telos'*, the final cause is specifically the ultimate purpose or end served by something – for the sake of which it exists in the first place.

To appraise the concept of God, the cosmological argument emphasizes on causal connections between objects, which are deemed crucial to their very existence. In doing so, it raises the following question: if everything has a cause, then what is the cause of the Universe? This is answered by introducing God as an uncreated substance or "uncaused cause" – to which all of Creation can trace its roots. As an integral part of the theory, God is defined as the First Cause, or the original cause, prior to which nothing existed. After close evaluation, however, the idea appears to be self-contradictory with a conclusion that is, to a large extent, limited. This is because, if we are to apply this theory in future, a First Cause would entail a Last Cause – in other words, every beginning has an end, which is yet to come. Without experiencing the end, therefore, it is unreasonable to assume that God is indeed the uncaused cause, when it could just as well be the Universe itself. In this regard, the argument collapses when placed in the future, paving way for "infinite regress". Moreover, by emphasizing on causal connections, the theory also sheds light on 'intentionality', which is the ability to refer to something that exists beyond consciousness. If we go by the logic of cause-and-effect relationships, assuming that God exists beyond the Universe, then the theory does not hypothesize what could possibly exist beyond God. While many critics of the argument consider this to be a fundamental flaw within the theory, defenders argue that it is only because we perceive God that His existence is determined – just as our existence is determined by His perceiving us, also known as "subjective idealism".

Although not many scholars accept the cosmological argument as an ultimate proof of God's existence, it was nevertheless supported by some of the greatest philosophers in history, including Plato and Aristotle. In particular, Plato's theory of Forms adds considerably to the idea of God being the uncaused cause. The theory interprets all forms of the sublime to be a representation of Divine Beauty or Absolute Perfection, meaning that they can ultimately be traced to an Ideal or original Form. Everything else is considered to be a mere reflection of the Ideal, reminding the subject of its familiarity with Absolute Perfection. Plato specifically discusses the theory of Forms with reference to love, adding that the love one feels for another human being is a reflection of one's love for Ideal Beauty. In doing so, he expounds on the idea that whatever beauty we perceive in this world is only but a glimpse of Absolute Beauty which exists in the metaphysical realm. Our longing to possess such beauty (or our attraction to it) simply reveals our inherent desire to seek union with the Ideal.

If we apply the theory of Forms to the cosmological argument, then perhaps we can surmise that the beauty of the Universe, in turn, reflects Ideal Beauty or Absolute Perfection that exists beyond our consciousness. This hints toward the existence of a single Truth or Reality that defines our own existence.

The third proposition in favor of God's existence is the Ontological Argument. Here, 'ontology' refers to the study of 'being'. This argument was most notably presented in the 11th century by St. Anselm as a scholastic justification for God in Christian theology. According to the argument, God is, first and foremost, clearly defined as a Supreme Being who possesses the attributes of omnipotence, omniscience and absolute goodness. This is to confirm that the conceptual image of God is one and the same, agreed by all to be necessarily and universally true – even for those who reject God. That is to say, the idea of God is part of *a priori* knowledge, as discussed in the introduction. Once this is established, the theory highlights that the concept of God is embedded in perfection and, since we are imperfect beings, the concept of perfection should technically be alien to us. The fact that we are familiar with it, despite our imperfection, only means that we have somehow witnessed it prior to our birth, or been purposely foretold of its existence by One who embodies perfection. As such, the argument suggests that perfection entails existence, which in turn substantiates the existence of God.

The cosmological argument was also famously advocated by 16th century philosopher, René Descartes (1596-1650), who expressed his views in a popular compilation of writings titled *"Meditations on First Philosophy"*. He composed different versions of the argument for the existence of God, all very much in line with St. Anselm's justification. According to Descartes, non-existence is a mark of imperfection, and if we are to conceive God in the image of perfection, then doubting His existence is essentially a massive contradiction on our part. He considered Plato's theory of Forms to explain his philosophy:

"Suppose, for example, that I have a mental image of a triangle. While it may be that no figure of this sort does exist or ever has existed outside my thought, the figure has a fixed nature (essence or form), immutable and eternal, which hasn't been produced by me and isn't dependent of my mind."

— Descartes, "Meditation V: On the Essence of Material Objects".

Critics of the cosmological argument commonly highlight a 'category mistake' within the proposition, which is a term coined by Gilbert Ryle to describe instances when *"things of one kind are presented as another"*. Renowned philosopher of the 18th century, Immanuel Kant (1724-1804), particularly criticized the cosmological argument for fundamentally reducing attributes such as 'perfection' to existence. According to Kant, existence is a predicate, because of which it can never be a property of an object or entity – if anything, an object or entity must first exist, if it is to have any attributes at all. Building on this argument, he reiterates that God cannot exist by virtue of His perfection, for that would mean reducing the scope of existence to perfection alone and, in doing so, dismissing other attributes for the purpose of justification.

Another critique of the argument was presented in the same century by a widely celebrated historian and philosopher, David Hume (1711-1776), who suggested that, though perfect ideals can certainly be conceived by the human mind, mere thoughts do not necessitate their existence. He exemplified his view through the concept of a perfect island, listing specific details which make the island perfect in every way. No matter how strongly we perceive this concept, we cannot prove that there is, in fact, a perfect island existing somewhere beyond our knowledge by simply imagining it. In a nutshell, the refutation highlights an absurd consequence of accepting the cosmological argument, rendering it illogical and, therefore, unconvincing.

While it is interesting to consider the three major philosophical debates concerning the existence of God, there are a number of areas often left largely unexplored, thus leaving much to one's personal interpretation to determine the nature of reality. In many cases, our decision to accept or reject God's existence can also be influenced by those around us, such as our family, friends, peers, role models or public figures. This is because many of us are likely to follow in the footsteps of those we look up to. It must be added, however, that coercion and reinforcement play a huge role in the conditioning and indoctrination of most religious ideologies, and although there may be instances in which children are raised to choose their own religious beliefs, they are comparatively few in number.

Consequently, atheism surfaces, in most cases, as a rational response to the injustices perpetuated in the name of religion. It is also common to adopt atheism as a means to rebel against authority or take control of one's life and, by doing so, assume responsibility for one's actions. This is primarily because a belief in God entails a belief in predestination and fate, a concept that may be disconcerting for some individuals who seek absolute control of their lives. For atheists, in particular, the subtle interplay between free will and destiny ultimately manifests as a major obstacle in life because it is assumed that the will of God supersedes the will of Man, and that everything in motion is in accordance with the Divine plan, which ultimately restricts our personal freedoms. There is no surprise, therefore, that much of atheism is intertwined with the idea of seeking liberation, whether it is from dictatorial rule in politics or government, or from any kind of exploitation triggered through religious norms.

3

ETYMOLOGY AND ORIGINS OF ATHEISM:

Atheism, in its modern sense, gained momentum most notably in the 18th century through philosophers such as David Hume and Immanuel Kant, among several other advocates of British empiricism. The origins of atheism, however, can be traced all the way back to ancient Greece wherein the term was known as *"atheos"*, loosely translated to mean "godless". In that particular era, the word bore exclusively negative connotations, used as a derogatory term for those who strongly opposed or disrespected one or more of the Greek gods – all the while placing their faith in other deities. It was not until fifth century BCE that the word 'atheist' was used to describe those who willfully deny the existence of all gods. Even then, however, it was not used personally by rebels to describe their own religious beliefs (or the lack thereof). Epicurus (300 BCE) was among the leading philosophers in ancient

Greece who contemplated the possibility that, despite their power and existence, the gods do not partake in any of the matters concerning the world. 'The Epicurean paradox', in particular, is largely credited for foreshadowing the crux of atheism, positing a trilemma about the nature of evil:

"Is God willing to prevent evil, but not able?
Then he is not omnipotent.
Is he able, but not willing?
Then he is malevolent.
Is he both able and willing?
Then whence cometh evil?
Is he neither able nor willing?
Then why call him God?"

— **Epicurus** ***(attributed).***

An iconic poet and philosopher hailing from Rome, Lucretius (95-55 BC) also added to the subject by being one of the founding fathers of 'naturalism', which is as an essential philosophical underpinning of modern-day atheism. As such, naturalism is heavily influenced by 'physicalism' which defines reality as a construction of material objects, thereby rejecting the possibility of a spiritual realm where immaterial objects and/or entities may exist. By postulating that everything is ultimately created from physical matter, physicalism contributes to atheism by demanding physical proof of God's existence. Although not all atheists are necessarily physicalists by nature, they are nevertheless inclined towards naturalism, which takes after physicalism in many ways. Naturalism espouses the thought that there is nothing beyond the natural world, thus suspending belief in the supernatural.

Since its origins, the term 'atheism' was synonymous with debauchery and ungodliness, seeing as the concept of God was generally inseparable from the tenets of ethics and morality. To reject God, therefore, was to reject the very foundations of moral conduct. In the 16th and 17th century, this impression of atheism remained intact until freethinkers and philosophers began advocating it to break free from the shackles of tyrannical rule, especially in response to the Catholic Church. This paved way for the Enlightenment Era, wherein revolutionaries followed in the footsteps of Copernicus and Galileo to oppose the dogmatic rule of conservative religious zealots in favor of science and reason.

It is believed that arguably the first book ever written with the intention to openly present the case of atheism was penned by French Catholic priest, Jean Meslier (1664–1729). Discovered upon his death, the book was published posthumously in the form of a detailed philosophical essay, which blatantly denied the concept of God (as described in, both, Abrahamic faith and Deism), along with rejecting the concept of the soul, miracles and the entire discipline of theology. In response to the association between God and morality, Meslier wrote:

"Whether there exists a God or not [...] men's moral duties will always be the same so long as they possess their own nature".

— ***Testament, Chapter V.***

Much of his writings reflected a deep-seated animosity towards the nobility and priests of the Catholic Church, whom he described as the root of social injustice. According to him, the only way to eliminate traces of evil was to call upon the execution of these specific individuals. This resentment, he stated, was not driven by revenge or hatred, but by a passion to elevate the principles of love and brotherhood. He expressed his views through a famous quote in which he refers to a man who*"...wished that all the great men in the world and all the nobility could be hanged, and strangled with the guts of the priests."* ***(Testament, Chapter II)***.

With regard to his writings, renowned philosopher, Michel Onfray, states that Meslier's work marks the beginning of *"the history of true atheism"*. Due to an onslaught of persecution against atheists within that period, however, it was imperative that such writings were published anonymously, which inevitably became common practice in the Age of Enlightenment.

4
ATHEISM AND THE ENLIGHTENMENT:

Some of the greatest contributions in atheism were made by the revolutionary frontrunners of the Enlightenment Era (15th–17th century), many of whom paved way for continental rationalism. This era was the dawning of Auguste Comte's third stage of consciousness – the first being willful submission to an invisible entity (or entities), the second being a metaphysical exploration of religious beliefs, and the third, a complete rejection of God (or gods) due to a lack of empirical evidence and application of scientific reason.

These were termed the three stages of law, as defined below:

> *"The law is this; that each of our leading conceptions, each branch of our knowledge, passes successively through three different theoretical conditions: the Theological, or fictitious; the Metaphysical, or abstract; and the Scientific, or positive."*
>
> — **Comte, *"Course of Positive Philosophy"*, 1830.**

In the wake of modernism, freethinkers the likes of Voltaire and Jean-Jacques Rousseau stood against the prejudice and subjugation of the Catholic Church by appealing to reason and scientific logic. The rebellion was also favored particularly by those experimenting in the field of science, such as Isaac Newton, who believed it was necessary to consider, at the very least, the propositions made by scientific experiments, which could help people evaluate their lives and discover what might exist beyond them. It is worth noting that Newton himself never claimed to deny the existence of God, but rather hypothesized that science could aid in the exploration of Christian theology. Consequently, they sparked a revolution in a mutual effort to overcome religious subjugation and the suppression of scientific discoveries. Since the radicalism of science threatened the power and influence of the Catholic Church, any ideas that contradicted the teachings of the Church were shunned outright. In order to maintain a stronghold, therefore, the King – who was believed to be appointed by God Himself – violently persecuted anyone who chose to rebel against him. What was to be a battle between dictatorship and freedom, ultimately surfaced as a battle between religion and science for it was the ultimate conflict between these instruments which came to define the Age of Enlightenment.

The censorship of irreligious sentiments further instigated hostility between believers and non-believers. More than anything else, however, it clearly portrayed religion as a force intolerant of other views and opinions, which is a fundamental deterrent for progress in any society. As a result, it only confirmed the suspicion that religious authorities did not want people exercising their "God-given" free will and choice to take control of their own lives. While supporters of the Enlightenment opposed the dogmatic teachings of the Catholic Church, many retained belief in other forms of higher power which gave birth to modern-day deism and pantheism. Voltaire is commonly recognized for shedding light on both beliefs, stating:

> *"What is faith? Is it to believe that which is evident? No. It is perfectly evident to my mind that there exists a necessary, eternal, supreme, and intelligent being. This is no matter of faith, but of reason."*
>
> **— Voltaire, *"Dictionnaire philosophique" (Philosophical Dictionary)*, 1764.**

This added considerable dimension to atheism as it was redefined into something more than a mere negation of theism. Many theologians argued that the very existence of atheistic ideology depended largely on the prevalence of theism. However, much of this criticism was countered by stretching the parameters of atheism to include multidimensional propositions. One of the propositions made was the possibility of the Universe being governed by a system of universal laws unintelligible to the human mind, as opposed to being controlled by "an old bearded man in the skies". The idea resonated with many atheists who, despite rejecting the existence of God, maintained the supposition that there is an inconceivable higher power that does not intervene in the matters of Creation.

This ideology was ultimately given the term 'deism' and Voltaire was believed to be a staunch enthusiast of this branch of philosophy.

He was, also, inadvertently responsible for founding "pantheism", the belief that the entire Universe encompasses a divinity which is essentially the driving force behind all Creation. It rejects the notion of a personal, anthropomorphic God, albeit reserving faith in the laws of Nature which are largely incomprehensible to humanity. French philosopher of the 16th century, Baruch Spinoza, provided deep insight into this framework, having a huge hand in countering Judeo-Christian teachings. His work posthumously came to light much later, having been published years after his death.

By the 18th century, philosophers who supported the epistemology of British empiricism, in turn, popularized the doctrine of skepticism which denies the possibility of certainty in knowledge. Thus, by continually doubting one's own existence, the question of God's existence became the center of philosophical discussions. This gave rise to a range of rational arguments against the existence of God, which corroborated the use of skepticism and reason to justify and confirm the claims. Some of the leading names in British empiricism, such as David Hume, supported the argument against God by laying emphasis on a lack of empirical evidence. This allowed atheists to embrace the title given to them, and eliminate the various negative connotations attached to it by appealing to intellect and rationalism.

With the popularity of this debate, atheists would even argue that it was a greater concern for believers to prove the existence of God, than for non-believers to disprove it. This was very much in line with the scientific school of thought, which laid more emphasis on observation and experimentation than anything else to verify hypotheses. Accordingly, atheists made their case stronger by proposing that one cannot determine the existence of an object without first observing the unknown phenomena, conducting experiments to test the hypothesis and finally presenting the conclusion with substantial evidence. The argument was greatly embedded in empiricism, which seeks to attain knowledge solely through sense perception and experience, as opposed to intuition and/or revelation alone – consequently bringing us back to the aforementioned conflict between *a priori* and *posteriori* knowledge. However, the argument was vehemently opposed by those who disagreed with the proposition of naturalism (also known as eliminative materialism). In response, opponents of atheism claimed that the world could certainly be composed of immaterial objects, and that we cannot disavow their intangible existence just because we lack the capacity to see them physically.

George Berkeley (1685-1753) is cited as one of the most influential people involved in the undertaking of immaterialist philosophy. He was responsible for the development of "subjective idealism", which resulted as a response to eliminative materialism. According to Berkeley, everything exists in relation to being perceived and, therefore, everything is essentially created from immaterial objects. He coined the phrase *"esse est percipi"* ("to be, is to be perceived") in order to illustrate his point, adding that reality is actively constructed through ideas and mental states. In doing so, he proposed that God exists simply because we perceive Him, just as we are able to exist through His perceiving us.

Immanuel Kant, however, rejected the notion of immaterialism and introduced, what he called, "transcendental idealism" in response to Berkeley's subjective idealism. Although he made several revisions in his philosophy, he made it clear that he considered Hume's skepticism to be deeply disturbing for it was an idea that awoke him from *"dogmatic slumbers"*. After spending twelve years in contemplation of this idea, he came to the conclusion that reality could also be defined through synthetic experience, which he used to explain his concept of 'transcendental idealism':

> *"Everything intuited or perceived in space and time, and therefore all objects of a possible experience, are nothing but phenomenal appearances, that is, mere representations, which in the way in which they are represented to us, as extended beings, or as series of changes, have no independent, self-subsistent existence apart from our thoughts. This doctrine I entitle 'transcendental idealism'."*
>
> — Kant, *"Critique of Pure Reason"*.

According to this definition, Kant effectively fused idealism with rationalism to describe the nature of reality, and thus dispelled Berkeley's idea of immaterialism. In addition, he used transcendental idealism to affirm the precedence of sense perception and experience over intuition and revelation in matters pertaining to the Unknown. His approach revealed a strong inclination towards reason as the main grounds to attest the validity of hypotheses in order to ensure their objectivity. Although Kant himself did not claim to be an atheist, he simply insisted on affirming that there was no way to empirically validate the existence of God. Due to the nature of this truth, he was compelled to shift his focus from proving this hypothesis and emphasized, instead, on the human capacity to perceive reality and interpret it as closely as possible to, what could possibly be, Absolute Reality.

The Age of Enlightenment created waves of change in the field of philosophy, urging people to adopt rationalism as a means to attain liberty and independence from oppressive rule. Kant had a massive influence on the spread of rationalism, having written a philosophical essay regarding the movement, which he titled *"Answering the Question: What is Enlightenment?"* The essay defined Enlightenment as a process whereby people engage in critical reasoning, and assess reality in terms of what they perceive on a personal level. It encouraged the idea of using logic and reason to decide "what ought to be", rather than being dictated by an external force such as religion, political leadership or the Church. This became the hallmark of Cartesian philosophy, especially when coupled with Kant's transcendental idealism.

5

KARL MARX, NIETZSCHE AND "THE DEATH OF GOD":

Around the 19th century, the scope of atheism expanded considerably to include the controversial theories of nihilism, liberalism and ultimately, "the death of God". Prominent advocates of atheism in this particular era were Karl Marx, Friedrich Nietzsche and Percy Bysshe Shelley, among several others. As discussions on the subject became increasingly popular, a diverse range of scholars and philosophers rose to fame as they delved into many different theories about atheism, each one taking on a different aspect of the ideology.

One of the most groundbreaking interpretations of the phenomenon was made by Karl Marx (1818-1883), who is most famously noted for describing religion as *"the opium of the people"* – an instrument that is used effectively to sedate and, hence, enslave the masses. In his point of view, religion was simply a drug created by the elite for the sole purpose of exploitation. By following the "divide and conquer" stratagem, it presented religion as a device used to boost the system of capitalism and produce a race of submissive slaves, incapable of thinking critically – let alone revolting against the system. Marx asserted that political history was defined by a constant class struggle between the *proletariat* (working class) and the *bourgeoisie* (aristocrats) – a conflict which religion helped to maintain. The speculation seemed to convince many, considering the fact that labor workers were severely distracted by religious debates. At the end of the day, people were too busy waging (religious or anti-religious) wars with each other to stand united against those in power.

Moreover, Nietzsche (1844–1900) added to atheism by exploring modernism in the context of religious breakdown. He postulated that rationalism and modern thought played a significant role in the collapse of organized religion, emphasizing that it is what caused religious foundations to crumble. Subsequently, he coined the aphorism *"Got ist tot"* (German for "God is dead") due to an increase in the de-Christianization of social values and norms. A number of anti-theistic movements spurred from the emergence of this idea as it indicated a moral breakdown of the Western world. Nietzsche elaborated his philosophy by suggesting that, without God or religion as our moral compass, humanity has spiraled into vortex of meaningless existence. This lack of purpose and meaning, he attributed to "the death of God" – a phenomenon that soon came to be known as 'nihilism'. He wrote several books on the idea, describing the gist of the matter in a section titled "The Madman":

"God is dead. God remains dead. And we have killed him. Yet his shadow still looms. How shall we comfort ourselves, the murderers of all murderers? What was holiest and mightiest of all that the world has yet owned has bled to death under our knives: who will wipe this blood off us? What water is there for us to clean ourselves? What festivals of atonement, what sacred games shall we have to invent? Is not the greatness of this deed too great for us? Must we ourselves not become gods simply to appear worthy of it?"

— Nietzsche, *"The Gay Science"*, Section 125.

Despite being responsible for the inception of this ideology, Nietzsche was very much aware of the repercussions of introducing nihilism in a society that was already on the brink of collapse. He feared for the fate of humanity if it were to accept this reality, since it left no room for redemption or growth. As a result, he called for an urgent reformation of old values – a process that he termed "transvaluation", urging for the creation of new ones that would restore the livelihood of humanity. He made cryptic references to the *Übermensch* (German for "overman" or "superman"; or, "superhuman" or "overhuman") in many of his writings, which was a goal he set for all of humanity to overcome its misery without turning to the deception of religion. He described it in the following words:

"Behold, I teach you the overman! The overman is the meaning of the earth. Let your will say: the overman shall be the meaning of the earth! I beseech you, my brothers, remain faithful to the earth, and do not believe those who speak to you of otherworldly hopes! Poison-mixers are they, whether they know it or not. Despisers of life are they, decaying and poisoned themselves, of whom the earth is weary: so let them go!"

— Nietzsche, *"Thus Spoke Zarathustra"*, *Prologue* §3.

The idea of the *Übermensch* was Nietzsche's solution to the moral decay of society, which he believed was the sole byproduct of religious imposition. In his view, much of humanity's discontent resulted from people's blatant disconnection from Nature – thus the concept of "the overman" was Nietzsche's way of reviving the sacredness of this connection. According to his perspective, it was necessary to devise a system of beliefs which, rather than instilling greed for another life based on perfection, encouraged people to accept this life as the only one they would ever have, since he found it more important for humanity to come to terms with the notion of death. It was only after accepting this reality that, in his opinion, people could consciously work to improve their lives and strive to make the world a better place. Moreover, he believed it was important to adhere to an ideology that opposed Platonic idealism, so that humanity could make an effort to do good for the sake of good, rather than out of lust for a perfect metaphysical realm which could otherwise compensate for a mundane existence on Earth.

With the passage of time, Nietzsche's thoughts shaped the course of existentialism which soon came to be recognized as 'nihilist existentialism'. The ideas conveyed through this school of thought were more or less centered on deconstructing the meaning of life, later to be considered a hallmark of modern atheism. By exploring the purposelessness of existence, nihilist existentialism purported that religion developed essentially out of humanity's inherent fear of death and desire for an afterlife. To overcome this fear, therefore, it was imperative to shift people's attention away from an afterlife towards finding or creating a purpose in earthly life – a purpose that was fundamentally subjective and personal to each individual.

Ultimately, nihilist existentialism paved way for the creation of postmodernism, a sociological paradigm that denies the existence of a standard and objective Truth or Reality for all. In doing so, it allowed people to create or define their own meaning of "God" – who or what it could possibly mean – and giving them the freedom to decide for themselves if such an entity even exists.

6

THE PARADOX OF ATHEISM AND WITTGENSTEINIAN FIDEISM:

In the 20th century, atheism gained considerable attention from some of the most important names in, what was soon to be, modern philosophy. Many of these supporters pioneered in their respective fields of expertise, thus adding to the credibility of their propositions. Bertrand Russell (1872-1970), for one, was hugely responsible for drawing parallels between the ideology of atheism and agnosticism, claiming that he belonged to both schools of thought. Although he maintained that there was no God, he also agreed with the Cartesian claim that there was no way to validate this speculation, thus rendering the debate futile. Moreover, he believed that new ideological frameworks such as communism were also nothing more than forms of religion in that they imposed an organized system of belief upon the masses – much like the belief in God. He contested that, in doing so, the perception of God as a sentient Being was simply being replaced with the notion of communism as a utopian ideal, and that the alternative did not offer anything more than what religious institutions did, despite advocating atheism.

Ultimately, he deduced that the only thing that could possibly change the course of humanity was co-operation between believers and non-believers since religion, indeed in any form, only sought to dictate and convolute people's perception of reality.

The reason why many of the greatest thinkers stood on the fence about making absolute judgments regarding the existence of God was because of an inability to prove either statement. In many cases, philosophers the likes of Russell agreed that, were we even to have tangible proof of God, the idea nevertheless instilled a sense of fear and dependency within people, which was counterproductive to their existence. In his point of view, such reckless fear was responsible for the dramatic increase in wars and misery around the world, and it would continue to do so until people collectively decided to overcome this fear. Inevitably so, he was influenced by Nietzsche's views which were echoed fervently in his writings, especially concerning the notion of death. Eventually, the debate was no longer centered on whether or not

God exists, but more importantly on how to move on with life, knowing that we may never empirically justify our assumption.

Popularly known for his philosophical analysis of language, Ludwig Wittgenstein (1889-1951) was also an active proponent of this thought. He made philosophical history by asserting that religious discourse is empirically untestable – therefore, to demand an empirical valuation of religious ideas is to demand the virtually impossible. In particular, Wittgenstein highlighted metaphysical and supernatural dimensions in religious discourse, emphasizing on the need to identify them in order to gain a better understanding of religious ideology. He felt there was a great weight of responsibility placed specifically on philosophers of religion as they were to provide an accurate translation of religious discourse. Absolute, unbiased clarity was essential in making religious interpretations for those who could not comprehend it. It was equally important, in his eyes, for such philosophers to withhold all judgments about religion when partaking in interpretive matters – where even the slightest imprecision could do colossal damage to the original message intended by religious scriptures.

According to Wittgenstein, humanity's intrinsic desire to prove or disprove religious postulations was a grave injustice to the theoretical framework of religious thought. This is because he believed that religion came with its own form of logic and life which could only be perceived in its own right, and was therefore fundamentally irreducible to empiricist epistemology. To impose science, or indeed any standard, upon religious discourse was to convert it into something else entirely. Just as science could be understood in its own language game, Wittgenstein claimed religion, too, could only be perceived in totality through a language game of its own, which was essentially distinct from other types. He explained that conflict is inevitable when people attempt to understand one language game in terms of another, which is reminiscent of understanding French through English subtitles. In other words, people may comprehend the words, but the translation would be void of depth, meaning and historical richness. This was termed "Wittgensteinian fideism", a philosophical reflection on the conflicting discourse of religion and science.

Despite the soundness of this proposition, critics of Wittgenstein's philosophy argue that if every discourse comes with its own form of life and logic, then essentially there is no way for us to evaluate it externally. Fideism refuses to address whether or not there is a standard form of life for religious discourse, or if they differ for various denominations – in which case, what are they, and how are we to determine the differences between them? To take an example, if we are to understand Christianity in its own right, then the question arises: should we apply the Christian language game for all denominations within Christianity, or would it vary for Presbyterianism, Protestantism, Lutheranism, Catholicism, and so forth? Moreover, fideism fails to explain how one should approach beliefs that are based on nothing more than intuition. In his book *"Atheism: A Philosophical Justification"*, Michael Martin addresses this problem by asking how anyone can criticize beliefs such as palm-reading or fortune-telling since, in defense of fideism, any critique posed would only be countered by one's lack of familiarity with the respective language game. The conjecture, therefore, leaves no possible room for criticism.

Noam Chomsky (born in 1928), an American linguist and philosopher, became a significant cultural figure in the 20th century, retaining his influence in the 21st century. Deeply inspired by Wittgenstein's philosophy of language, he incorporated it into many of his own writings on subjects pertaining to war, political history and the mass media. He has contributed to Wittgensteinian fideism by suggesting that religious discussions almost always result in conflict largely due to miscommunication and preconceived notions. In his view, unless people are able to develop a universally acceptable definition of what qualifies as religion or God, it is unreasonable for us to expect a clear exchange of dialogue or ensure a smooth transfer of knowledge. Regarded widely as an atheist, or more prominently as a *"child of the Enlightenment"*, Chomsky is often asked in interviews about his reasons for being an atheist, to which he is reported to have replied:

> *"I don't even know what an atheist is. When people ask me if I'm an atheist, I have to ask them what they mean. What is it that I'm supposed to not believe in? Until you can answer that question I can't tell you whether I'm an atheist, and the question doesn't arise. [...] I don't see how one can be an agnostic when one doesn't know what it is that one is supposed to believe in, or reject."*

— Chomsky, *"Science on the Dock"*, 2006.

Evidently, Chomsky influenced the socio-politico dimensions of religious discourse, encouraging people to evaluate what they mean when they speak of "God", or how it is possible to absolutely denounce or accept the existence of that which cannot be heard, seen, felt or touched. Contextually, the greatest concern is not whether one accepts or rejects the notion of God, but one's inability to perceive the totality of the Unknown. Similarly, if one claims to have experienced a reality of that magnitude, then the issue which stems henceforth is how to express this reality through language, which is a characteristically limited medium. Any attempts to explain it, therefore, would be ultimately flawed and imprecise, adding nothing substantial to our knowledge of the Unknown.

Many atheists agreed with this hypothesis, asserting the need to define God, while others assumed Nietzsche's speculation about the death of God, citing it as the reason for our inability to define such an entity in absolute terms. In the 1960's, the "Death of God" movement became a popular discussion among the masses, especially when it was mentioned in an issue of *TIME* Magazine, featuring the title, *"Is God dead?"* The issue received a massive backlash from readers, many of whom regarded the cover to be *"a haven of godlessness"*, despite the content being a philosophical exploration of the rise and fall of Christian dogmatism in the Western world. The movement stemmed from the belief that God was no longer relevant in the modern world and that it was safe to assume, therefore, that He was 'dead'.

It was a matter of opinion for different theologians whether God was ever alive, or if His death was purely figurative in the sense that it lost meaning and purpose with time. Some believed that it was faith that gave Him life, adding that God could be revived if we were to renew our faith in Him. The most striking interpretation, however, was made by Thomas J. J. Altizer, Professor at Emory University, who suggested that God was once, in fact, alive – fully embodied through Jesus Christ – but during the crucifixion of Christ, His spirit had abandoned the physical world. The suggestion met with raving criticism by Christians who considered the idea blasphemous and highly offensive.

With regards to the "death of God" theology, renowned poet and writer in the 20th century, T. S. Eliot (1888-1965) highlighted that such movements could not be considered a serious contribution to atheism in any way. He contested that the suggested ideas focused exclusively on Christianity, ignoring the 'death' of

God in other religions. For instance, to explain his agnostic and atheist beliefs, Bertrand Russell wrote a book which he titled, *"Why I am not a Christian"*, regarded by Eliot as a perfect example of his argument. He explained that people who believe in the death of God, having been raised Christian, could not seriously be considered atheists since they had only abandoned the notion of God in one religion. Such people could eventually just as well find themselves becoming Buddhist, Hindu or Muhammadan since they did not know enough about God to reject Him completely. According to Eliot, it was only Christianity they had abandoned, not the totality of God or religion as a universal phenomenon.

7

NEW ATHEISM AND THE SECULAR WORLD:

Without concrete proof of a Creator, atheists choose to deny His existence entirely, especially since many of the world's greatest crimes and sins are often committed in the name of God or legitimized through (a distortion of) religious doctrines. Furthermore, they argue that the socio-politico implications of believing in God are not only disruptive for foreign relations – since history reveals that one man's terrorist could be another man's freedom-fighter – but it also allows for a perversion of human values under the pretext of religious freedom. Many of the greatest wars have been fought with religious motives in mind, and many political ambitions, pursued in the guise of religious emancipation.

Following the 9/11 attacks on the World Trade Center and the Pentagon, there was an instantaneous revival of atheism in the Western world which spread sporadically in the 21st century. As a result, atheists were able to voice their opinions more openly than ever before, pressing the government and public to accept it as an undeniable repercussion of promoting religious ideology. Today, many of them make their case by asserting that the attacks were religiously-motivated, and therefore, demonstrate how far people are willing to go in the name of "God". In doing so, atheists attempt to justify atheism by presenting 9/11 as a devastating aftermath of espousing belief in religion or a God. However, defenders of religious institutions debate that religion, much like any other tool (such as the media, for instance), can be distorted for sinister purposes, which is primarily why the solution for wars, inequality and bloodshed does not lie in eliminating religion entirely. They add that to do so would be to fundamentally restrict people's religious freedoms, which is a breach of their basic human rights. Therefore, imposing a restriction of this magnitude would only cause a dramatic backlash, instigating further hostility between believers and non-believers.

Due to the radicalization of various religions, however, several atheists have risen to fame by claiming that it is no longer acceptable to live in a world which refuses to expose the deception and bigotry of religious thought. Not only do they urge for a separation between religion and the state, but also feel it is their obligation to negate theism, countering and criticizing it wherever it gains momentum. This, they claim, is necessary to ensure the safety of all humanity, for it is a means to spread awareness about the potential dangers of such a belief. This dimension of anti-theistic sentiments came to be defined as "New Atheism", marking the evolution of atheism in the 21st century. Unlike atheists of the past, proponents of New Atheism focus on blatantly opposing religion and attacking it, which is described as being central to their ideology. They reiterate the need to overcome religious influence by means of rational arguments since that is the only way to maintain precedence over seemingly illogical hypotheses. Perhaps what makes New Atheism fundamentally different from the kind of atheism practiced prior to the 21st century is that it insists on eliminating any and all forms of tolerance towards religion, deeming it counterproductive to the cause of atheism.

Some of the most active supporters of New Atheism are Richard Dawkins (author of the best-selling book *"The God Delusion"*), Daniel Dennett, Sam Harris, and Christopher Hitchens, who are together popularly referred to as "The Four Horseman of New Atheism" – a satirical allusion to the *"Four Horseman of the Apocalypse"* mentioned in the Book of Revelation. The most characteristic feature of this movement is its deep inclination towards defying all religious doctrines as bitterly and vociferously as possible. Advocates of New Atheism are known primarily for their ability to compel other atheists into strictly opposing religious institutions, even if it means transgressing the boundaries of free-speech. They claim religious tolerance is no longer something that can or should be sustained in the modern world, blaming it for the overwhelming command of religious ideology.

Moreover, they assert the notion that religion should not be synonymous with morality, for to equate the two would be to claim that those who do not believe in God are fundamentally immoral. Much of modern-day atheism attempts to reform these assumptions and reinterpret morality as something that is essentially independent of religion. The idea seems to predate the philosophical arguments made by atheists in the 21st century, many of whom question what ethics and morality would mean in the absence of God. While not all atheists support "New Atheism" movements, they nevertheless believe it is important to have a separation between religion and the state. This school of thought has left a massive influence on social and political ideas such as secularism, religious pluralism and disestablishment. Although secularism, in particular, is not exclusive to atheism, it still remains a crucial part of its core philosophy.

The term 'secularism' was coined by George Jacob Holyoake (1817–1906) in the early 20th century. Deeply inspired by Auguste Comte's sociological insight, he paid close attention to Comte's Religion of humanity, described by John H. Huxley as *"Catholicism minus Christianity"*. Secularism itself, however, emerged as a political ideology which threatened the stronghold of religious supremacy, pertaining to a system of governance that is not influenced in any way by religious beliefs. Due to the negative connotations attached to atheism, however, Holyoake preferred to describe his political ideology as "secularism", discussing its theoretical framework as one that does not intend to damage or criticize religion, but rather works independently to restore the goodness of human life. This was in stark contrast to today's New Atheism, since it did not emerge as a means to end religious tolerance. It entwined its principles with those of science, deeming it an exemplary model from which humanity can seek to be noble and virtuous in a stable, developing society. The bedrock of this political ideology was defined by morality as an independent motive, unbarred by religious values or norms. Drawing upon these ideas, Holyoake explained:

> *"Secularism is a code of duty pertaining to this life, founded on considerations purely human, and intended mainly for those who find theology indefinite or inadequate, unreliable or unbelievable. Its essential principles are three: (1) The improvement of this life by material means. (2) That science is the available Providence of man. (3) That it is good to do good. Whether there be other good or not, the good of the present life is good, and it is good to seek that good."*

> — **Holyoake, *"English Secularism"*, 1896.**

Most commonly associated with French secularity of the 20th century, secularism also changed in definition with the passage of time. In the 20th century, it was popularly referred to as *"laïcité"*, a political attitude that maintained a strict division between religion and governmental affairs. The idea came to light in the French society during a conflict surrounding the removal of religious teachers in elementary schools. In 1958, The French Constitution set secularist ideas in motion by stating that *"The Republic neither recognizes, nor salaries, nor subsidizes any religion"*. Contemporary atheism makes the same demands from a truly democratic government, claiming it is imperative to adhere to a policy that is line with the secularization thesis. According to this, it is assumed that any society progressing through rationalization and modernization eventually weakens religious influence in the social and political arena.

Noam Chomsky is often noted for his keen insight on the subject as he draws interesting parallels between democratic secularism and religion as a social institution:

"Worship of the state has become a secular religion for which the intellectuals serve as priesthood. [...] The more primate sectors of Western culture go further, fostering forms of idolatry in which the sacred symbol of the flag becomes an object of forced veneration, and the state is called upon to punish any insult to them and to compel children to pledge their allegiance daily, while God and State are almost indissolubly linked in public ceremony and discourse."

— Chomsky, *"Deterring Democracy"*, 1992.

Chomsky's statement sheds light on the cultural symbolism behind religion in the modern world, evoking the phenomenological underpinnings of a truly democratic state. He invites people to consider how far a society can go in terms of removing religion from the public sphere, especially when the very essence of nationalism rests largely on a kind of devotion reminiscent of religious faith. Here, the analogy of 'secular religion' functions effectively as a control agent; the only difference being that it is veiled under the garb of foreign policy. In turn, people's obedience to elected leaders and their foreign-relations policy ultimately manifests as a distinct form of submission, many of whom are convinced that every action executed in the name of democracy must indeed have moral implications. This blind devotion mirrors the same religious devotion so strongly opposed by atheists, a feature found most commonly in the Western world where one's attitude towards patriotism is determined by one's loyalty towards the government. As such, a true citizen is expected to adhere to the word of law very much like the Gospel Truth.

Critics of New Atheism argue that, rather than progressing society, the movement aims to impose its ideology upon the masses, taking away people's right to religious freedom – an act that goes against the very foundations of liberalism and modernization. For others, the movement seems to misrepresent other atheists around the world who, while supporting the notion of secularism, do not rebuke those who advocate religious tolerance. Many critics even go on to speculate that the rise of New Atheism as a post-9/11 event suspiciously led to the birth of "Islamophobia", which is a form of prejudice or irrational hatred towards Muslims. William W. Emilson describes it specifically as an *"attack not only on militant Islamism but also on Islam itself under the cloak of its general critique of religion"*. Moreover, sociologist William Stahl emphatically stresses on the similarities that New Atheism ironically shares with a system it claims to oppose, stating, *"What is striking about the current debate is the frequency with which the New Atheists are portrayed as mirror images of religious fundamentalists."*

While today's atheism is not defined exclusively by New Atheism, it nevertheless indicates substantial growth from what it used to be in the pre-Socratic era. Contemporary atheism is more characteristic of a strictly secularist philosophy, making no particular demands for a dogmatic take-over except in areas pertaining to politics and foreign relations as they play a crucial role in reflecting national identity. Countries such as Turkey, India and France, for instance, have adopted a secularist policy, which atheists believe is an essential step towards developing a truly egalitarian society. It is common practice for atheists to reinstate these demands in countries that oppose secularism. Quite often it is done by highlighting the grave injustices faced by religious minorities in local areas. This is because a country's mainstream religion functions as the sole authority, eliminating anything that even remotely threatens its influence – whether it is intentional or unintentional. Accordingly, atheists believe secularism can provide a greater possibility of establishing a harmonious and peaceful society where people have the right to worship whoever or whatever they want, just as long as it does not interfere with matters pertaining to the state. The modern atheistic worldview, therefore, depends largely on the degree of tolerance exhibited by those who deny the existence of God.

8

ETYMOLOGY AND ORIGINS OF AGNOSTICISM

The foundations of agnosticism were famously laid down by Thomas Henry Huxley (1825–1895), an English biologist (scientist and philosopher) who was an active proponent of Charles Darwin's theory of evolution. He is remembered chiefly for coining the very term "agnosticism" to express his beliefs regarding the existence or non-existence of God and/or supernatural deities. In a time when propositions about the nature and scope of God's existence became the keystone of philosophical discussions, Huxley found himself growing increasingly certain of his own uncertainty, unable to identify or discover even a shred of evidence to justify plausible claims.

This nameless indecision in itself, however, predates the 19th century, having been the subject of contemplation for renowned philosophers in ancient

Greece, such as Pyrrho, Protagoras and – to an extent – even Socrates, who followed the skeptical approach to perceiving knowledge. Taking its roots in ancient Greek etymology, the term 'agnosticism' literally translates into "without knowledge". This is a quintessential paradox, highlighting a discrete and esoteric path to knowledge through an acceptance of ignorance within the self. Regarding the inception of agnostic thought, Huxley is quoted to have said:

"The one thing in which most of these good people were agreed was the one thing in which I differed from them. They were quite sure they had attained a certain "gnosis," – had, more or less successfully, solved the problem of existence; while I was quite sure I had not, and had a pretty strong conviction that the problem was insoluble. And, with Hume and Kant on my side, I could not think myself presumptuous in holding fast by that opinion. [...].

So I took thought, and invented what I conceived to be the appropriate title of "agnostic." It came into my head as suggestively antithetic to the "gnostic" of Church history, who professed to know so much about the very things of which I was ignorant. [...] To my great satisfaction the term took."

— Huxley, *"Collected Essays, Volume V: Science and Christian Tradition"*, 1893.

The term ultimately surfaced as a denial of absolute judgment, existing in close relation to Hume's hypothesis of doubt and skepticism in matters pertaining to the Unknown. This is primarily why people belonging to the field of neuroscience or psychology often use 'agnosticism' in reference to 'the unknowable'. While it may be true that agnostic thought was crafted largely by the pillars of indecision and uncertainty, it eventually emerged as a distinct belief system in its own right, without leaning towards any particular theological framework.

According to Huxley's definition, agnosticism is described as one's humble acceptance of the notion that one does not possess any knowledge about the Absolute Truth, which can also be considered conversely proportional to claiming absolute knowledge. It was brought to light publicly in a meeting at the Metaphysical Society in 1869, when Huxley openly discussed his religious thoughts in a speech written with the intention to introduce agnosticism to the public. His speech garnered the attention of several intellectuals, especially since it resonated with many of those who felt that their religious views did not coincide with preexisting philosophical sentiments. By giving these views a name and foundation, Huxley was able to draw parallels between Socratic wisdom and the idea of rejecting claims to absolute or metaphysical knowledge.

This is an interesting addition to detail considering that Socrates himself very much believed in a God, although he too withheld judgments about the rigidity and absoluteness of his claims. In doing so, Huxley did not intend to convert Socratic teachings into his own framework of philosophy, but simply meant to highlight many of the similarities between the two.

The subtle interplay between agnosticism and Socratic wisdom can be understood more deeply through an exploration of his famous quote:

"I am the wisest man alive, for I know one thing, and that is that I know nothing."

— **Socrates, (469-399 BC).**

According to Huxley, the wisdom contained therein reflects the crux of agnosticism, which is to humbly accept our ignorance of a Reality that far exceeds our knowledge. The paradoxical nature of enlightenment, as described by Socrates in the aforementioned quote, plays a pivotal role in encapsulating the very foundation of agnostic philosophy. This much can be deduced from the simple fact that agnosticism exists in contrast to the all-knowing presumptions of religious leaders who claim to have answers to all the perennial questions of life. In Huxley's perspective, to even make such a statement is to renounce the importance of seeking truth, since the very presumption of Absolute Reality limits us from entertaining the possibility of higher truths.

As such, the essence of agnosticism lies predominantly in the flexibility of one's belief. In other words, one must be open to all possibilities, even if they appear to go against everything internalized in the human mind. In this regard, the quest to seek absolute truth is given more weight than satisfying one's egotistical desire to know it all. This is because agnostics believe it is only by breaking down the barricades of pride and pre-conceived notions that one is prepared to digest realities greater than oneself, thus allowing one to truly evolve as a human being.

It is worth considering that Huxley's solution to evolving the state of humanity clearly echoed Socrates' emphasis on improving the Soul, back when religious dogma ran rampant in ancient Greece. While the origins of agnosticism lie chiefly in uncertainty and skepticism, the philosophical justification behind it is deemed fundamentally logical. That is to say, Huxley's perspective was grounded in Cartesian reason and Humian philosophy, thereby making his proposition philosophically potent. Accordingly, the agnostic view reiterates it is only after the acknowledgement of one's own ignorance that one is able to explore greater truths without any bias.

Agnosticism as the "reverse of atheism":

The concept of agnosticism often appears to be very much in keeping with the atheist school of thought in that they both originally advocate science or materialist philosophy to build upon hypotheses concerning the existence of God. It is worth noting, however, that agnosticism is defined by the suspension of belief when confronted with absolute conclusions – even if these conclusions are drawn from repeated experimentation and close observation. This divergence alone is strictly opposed to atheism as it holds such conclusions potentially falsifiable. Interestingly, this is also where agnosticism deviates from theism since it considers the religious stance on God's existence equally falsifiable. This stems from the problem of induction, made popular by Karl Popper (1902-1994), who initiated the falsification theory to specifically address the clause of uncertainty in scientific experiments.

While some may argue that agnosticism holds more in common with atheism than any other school of thought, philosopher William Stuart Ross interestingly referred to it as *"the very reverse of atheism"* by virtue of its open-endedness. Understandably, atheists do not enjoy being mistaken for or identified as agnostics since their stance on the existence of God is fortified and made resolute with reason, while the agnostic justification seems to challenge the rational validity of their claims. Atheists believe that being ostracized from society for denying God is a grave injustice in itself for it restricts their freedom to believe in what they want. Additionally, being misrepresented by agnostics makes their survival even more difficult as they refuse to support them despite acknowledging that God probably does not exist.

It is because of their "half here-half there" state of mind that agnostics cannot be merged or confused with atheists, since the resoluteness with which atheists deny God is perhaps their most characteristic feature. In which case, agnosticism can be considered to have about as much in common with theism as it does with atheism. However, it must be noted that by going against the very foundation of atheism, which is the absolute rejection of God, agnosticism is a complete reversal of the atheistic philosophy for it opens a window of vast interpretations regarding God's existence, all the while citing reason as its justification. After all, we must not forget that it was reason alone that compelled Huxley to question God's existence or non-existence, ultimately coming to the conclusion that we cannot know for certain what exists beyond the horizon of the Unknown:

"In matters of the intellect, follow your reason as far as it will take you, without regard to any other consideration. And negatively: In matters of the intellect, do not pretend that conclusions are certain which are not demonstrated or demonstrable."

— **Huxley, *"Agnosticism"*, 1889.**

Free-thinker of the Enlightenment, David Hume, known primarily for his focus on empiricism and reason, contended that the element of doubt and skepticism is crucial to the development of one's knowledge in all fields. He inadvertently contributed to the theory of agnosticism by discussing the concept of "tentative belief" which, to him, existed in almost every hypothesis. With the exception of tautologies (statements that are absolutely true by definition, such as "a three-sided triangle"), Hume asserted that practically everything is subject to doubt. This is simply because he acknowledged the fallibility of human beings when they attempt to determine the objective nature of reality.

Moreover, Søren Kierkegaard, famous for his views on existential philosophy, even went on to discourage philosophers from trying to validate or prove the existence of God through reason. From what he could gather, the very concept of a 'presupposition' suggested that ideas conceived before assumption (such as that of God) did indeed exist somewhere beyond our consciousness; which is to say, they were clearly part of *a priori* knowledge. However, to claim that such ideas can be proven through science was, in his opinion, making far-reaching statements out of arrogant and haste judgment, which goes against the very principles of scientific analysis.

Huxley was a man of reason, identified primarily as a scientist, who did not intend to initiate a cult through his stance on God, but rather explore reality with the aid of tangible, empirical evidence. While he did not reject or accept the existence of God, he maintained that science could not provide enough justification for either proposition, reiterating that even *"a scintilla of evidence"* would make him jump to an absolute conclusion, whether it was in favor of God's existence or an opposition to the claim. This indecision, he claimed, resulted through his exploration as a scientist more than anything else, and he urged others to withhold their judgments as well since justifying or proving the matter was clearly beyond our capacity as human beings. Many took this to mean humanity's humble submission to the laws of Nature since it is assumed that the perfection of cosmic order far overshadows humanity's imperfect knowledge of the world.

Famed politician and renowned orator of the 19th century, Robert G. Ingersoll was also one of the leading contributors in the philosophy of agnosticism, popularly known as the "Great Agnostic". While he acknowledged that the natural system is infinite and supreme, he added that there was no evidence to suggest divine intervention in matters concerning humanity. As such, Ingersoll believed that the idea of attributing worldly affairs to an arbitrary God was fundamentally void of reason and thus, did not adhere to the laws of science. It was important for scientists to make observations based on complete honesty to ensure their objectivity, and in matters pertaining to God or a higher power, Ingersoll stressed on accepting the absence of a conclusion rather than reinforcing the supremacy of science. In his agnostic declaration, he highlighted that metaphysical assumptions regarding God were contrary to the pillars of rational thought, addressing his views in the following words:

> *"Is there a God? I do not know. Is man immortal? I do not know. One thing I do know, and that is, that neither hope, nor fear, belief, nor denial, can change the fact. It is as it is, and it will be as it must be."*
>
> — **Ingersoll, *"Why I am an Agnostic"*, 1896.**

In this regard, perhaps what is most striking about agnosticism is the fact that it applies the same logic so strongly advocated by atheists, to justify a philosophical stance which happens to be vastly different from theirs. Consequently, atheists defend themselves against agnostic thought, rather than see eye to eye with it. In many cases, agnosticism is even criticized by staunch atheists for hiding behind the veil of uncertainty and failing to address many of the loopholes and ambiguities permeating through its philosophy.

One of the greatest criticisms faced by agnosticism is that it chooses to reserve judgment specifically in the case of God's existence, when it could just as well suspend judgment in other scenarios where there is no tangible evidence to confirm a particular hypothesis. To take an example, proponent of New Atheism, Richard Dawkins shares his views on the subject by claiming that he supports agnosticism to the extent that he is *"agnostic about fairies living in the bottom of the garden"*. This is a mockery of agnostic sentiments for, contextually, there is no way to confirm the proposition unless we were to dig to the bottom of the earth. Although no such pursuit for absolute knowledge has been recorded to date, it is still generally assumed that there is most probably no truth to this hypothesis. In which case,

Dawkins posits why matters pertaining to God's existence should be treated any differently.

In spite of that, however, he empathizes with agnostics who strive to attain the absolute truth rather than live their lives believing a potential lie. He terms this system of belief as 'Temporary Agnosticism in Practice' (TAP), for these agnostics choose to suspend judgment solely because of a lack of convincing or concrete evidence regarding God's existence or non-existence. On the other hand, he distinguishes such agnostics from those who are wholly convinced that the existence or non-existence of God can never be proven, not by themselves nor others. These people, according to Dawkins, undermine the potential and necessity of science because their permanent indecision reflects a paradoxical, almost self-contradictory approach to perceiving knowledge. Consequently, he identifies them as followers of 'Permanent Agnosticism in Principle' (PAP), ironically echoing the dogmatic papacy of the Catholic Church.

Moreover, Pope Benedict XVI asserted the dangers of espousing agnosticism as it places scientific truth superior to religious or philosophical truths. He explained that, rather than attempting to understand the concept of God, agnostics seek convenience and their beliefs encourage them to live in ignorance of a truth that could otherwise change the course of their life. In addition, Christian theologians contend to this day that the argument by which agnostics claim to justify their indecision could just as well be applied to gravity, reason and thought, since their existence is also intangible in nature.

In the 19th century, Charles A. Watts, an English secularist editor, went on to publish a magazine titled *"The Agnostic Annual"*, which discussed in great detail the rising influence of agnosticism. While the first few editions of the magazine accredited Huxley as "the founder of atheism", it is believed that he was not pleased with the assertion, preferring, instead, to be portrayed as a man who simply coined the term. Indeed Huxley had no interest in becoming famous for his unconventional views on God and religion, deeming it more important to be a responsible human being who sought simply to help others.

Russell's Teapot:

Bertrand Russell created a unique place for himself in the realm of religion and science, identifying himself as, both, an atheist and agnostic. Although certain boundaries are generally defined to separate atheism from agnosticism, Russell found himself unable to step over them as he saw an element of truth to both philosophical perspectives. As an atheist, he maintained his belief in the likelihood that there is no God (or gods) controlling the Universe, but felt equally compelled to add that he could not prove his personal conjecture. It was essentially due to a lack of evidence in favor of his hypothesis, that he was caught between the two schools of thought, unable to stick solely to one.

While atheists generally claim to have conclusive evidence for their disbelief in God, agnostics pass no judgment on such metaphysical speculations for they are convinced it cannot be empirically justified. Russell asserted that, for someone with his views on God or a supreme deity, there was no particular system of belief distinct from the two, which could be followed without overlapping with the fundamental features of atheism and/or agnosticism. He wrote a pamphlet titled *"Am I an Atheist or an Agnostic?"* to shed light on his dilemma, stating:

"As a philosopher, if I were speaking to a purely philosophic audience I should say that I ought to describe myself as an Agnostic, because I do not think that there is a conclusive argument by which one can prove that there is not a God. On the other hand, if I am to convey the right impression to the ordinary man in the street I think I ought to say that I am an Atheist, because when I say that I cannot prove that there is not a God, I ought to add equally that I cannot prove that there are not the Homeric gods."

— Russell, *"A Plea For Tolerance In The Face Of New Dogmas"*, 1947.

In an attempt to address the burden of proof faced by those who doubt the existence of God, Russell drew the analogy of a cosmic or celestial teapot, commonly known as "Russell's teapot". He postulated that, if he was to assume the existence of a china teapot orbiting the Sun between Earth and Mars in arbitrary motion, it would be nonsensical for him to expect others to agree just because the hypothesis could not be disproved. He fashioned the teapot after the conceptualized image of God, asserting the need to eliminate the philosophic burden of proof which was unnecessarily and quite absurdly placed on skeptics. According to him, the burden of proof should technically be placed on those who make unverified claims, such as religious devotees who believe in God's existence, rather than those who deny him.

In regards to the celestial teapot, Russell claimed that the notion of an all-encompassing Divinity beyond the cosmos should be treated the same as the notion of an assumed teapot, since that too cannot be proven – especially if he were to add that the teapot was too small to be observed even through the most powerful of telescopes. In doing so, he illustrated the deep-seated bias that orthodox Christians held against skeptics who questioned God's existence on the grounds of no empirical evidence. Through his analogy, he urged theists to honestly ask themselves how it would appear if their argument was used to prove the existence of a teapot in place of God – and if denying the existence of that teapot would be a debate of epic proportions.

Ultimately, Russell came to the conclusion that it was the dogmatic surge of religious influence which caused people to react negatively, even if the questions they were confronted with were perfectly reasonable. He summed up his views in the following words:

> *"If, however, the existence of such a teapot were affirmed in ancient books, taught as the sacred truth every Sunday, and instilled into the minds of children at school, hesitation to believe in its existence would become a mark of eccentricity and entitle the doubter to the attentions of the psychiatrist in an enlightened age or of the Inquisitor in an earlier time."*

— Russell, *"Is There a God?"* (1952).

Accordingly, Russell's teapot became a philosophical emblem of skeptic ideology, used frequently in debates pertaining to the existence of God. The analogy was also subject to several criticisms, many of which highlighted that it erroneously equated the grand conception of God, in all His infinite power, with something as insignificant and paltry as a mere teapot. As such, James Wood, an

English literary critic born in 1965, noted Russell's argument as being inherently biased towards the possibility of a God by attempting to draw parallels between two forms that held absolutely nothing in common. He felt the bias was encapsulated through the very fact that Russell chose to exemplify the expansiveness and omnipotence of God through a definitively small and relatively unimportant object.

In addition, the analogy was highly criticized by philosopher Eric Reitan, who indicated a fundamental flaw in Russell's proposition. Since a teapot is fundamentally physical in nature, Reitan claimed it was illogical to surmise that it could help us in evaluating the God debate. The very concept of God dictates an experiential process, for he believed God was essentially inscrutable to the physical eye which is what made the debate unlike any other.

Pascal's Wager:

Agnosticism, unlike atheism, was not subjugated as intensely and violently as atheism, although it took considerable time for society to accept it during the supremacy of religion, especially with the escalating power and prestige of the Catholic Church. In the 17th century, however, French philosopher and mathematician, Blaise Pascal (1623-1662) proposed a Christian apologetic for the existence of God, which ultimately came to be known as "Pascal's Wager". Apologetics were popularized by Christian theologians as a means to defend the Christian faith without causing offense to any other religion. Amid the rising influence of agnosticism, Pascal's wager became a useful argument to evaluate the finite losses and gains of believing in or rejecting God's existence.

In particular, Pascal presented a wager in his apologetic, illustrating two scenarios wherein the existence and non-existence of God played an active role in defining the purpose and lifestyle of humanity. The first scenario entailed living one's life according to the assumption that God exists, and ultimately discovering that the assumption is true. The second scenario entailed living according to the assumption that God exists and ultimately discovering that He does not. Pascal shed light on these scenarios, evaluating the moral implications of both. He argued that if one is to live by the principle of God's existence, it would mean living with moral consciousness, developing a sense of responsibility and contributing to the welfare of society. If it is ultimately discovered that God does indeed exist, the individual would have lived in accordance with God's will, and if He does not exist, then the individual would have lost nothing in the process, barring temporary finite pleasures. The underlying message of the wager is that belief in God is comparatively worthwhile as opposed to disbelief in God.

However, neither atheism nor orthodox Christians bought into Pascal's wager, since the greatest criticism faced by the proposition was the fact that it overlooked the concept of God in religions other than Christianity. Although Voltaire was born decades after this apologetic was released, his views on Pascal's wager shaped a striking argument against the dogmatic imposition of theism upon those who chose to deny God's existence. He considered it *"childish and immature"* to measure the pros and cons of believing in a potentially false hypothesis as it appeared to go against the fundamentals of scientific truth. According to him, the wager was nothing more than a fool's trick to convert non-believers or 'infidels' (as they were more commonly referred to) into practicing Christianity. Moreover, he highlighted that the wager did not take into account the consequences of its assertion.

Even if we were to accept God's existence according to Pascal's theory of finite pleasures, the wager still did not point specifically to the Christian

God, and therefore could be used to justify God's existence even in other Abrahamic religions such as Islam or Judaism. In other words, it would defy the logic laid down by orthodox Christians to justify the existence of the Christian God, thus causing them to criticize the wager. To others, it was simply a matter of choosing a more convenient route to life, many of whom felt that a reality of this magnitude should not be reduced to mere calculations and measurements.

Darwinism and Spencerism:

Charles Darwin (1809-1882) was an English naturalist, known primarily for giving birth to the theory of evolution. He maintained a close friendship with Huxley for a significant part of his life, to the extent that Huxley was often referred to as "Darwin's Bulldog". Incidentally, it was also Huxley who coined the term "Darwinism" to shed light on the scientific evolutionary theories of natural selection and genetic transmutation, originally written by Darwin in a book titled *"On the Origins of Species"*.

Raised in non-conformist Unitarianism, Darwin reserved a deep interest in the natural laws, particularly in Wesley's natural theology which coincided with the teachings of Christianity. Initially a devout believer of God, Darwin strongly agreed with the theory of creationism, as far as quoting verses from the Bible to espouse Christian virtues of morality. However, after returning from the Beagle expedition in the 1830's, he began questioning the historical accuracy of the Bible, in addition to wondering why all religions of the world were not given equal importance. While he retained belief in God as *"the ultimate law-giver"*, he studied adaptation and geology close enough to deduce that there was something beyond the design argument which could explain the origins of species.

In 1858, he published *"On the Origins of Species"* which is widely regarded as the bedrock of evolutionary biology. It was in this scientific literature that Darwin introduced the theory of natural selection to explain the fixed laws of nature and transmutation of species over time. While the evidence suggested human evolution as a criticism of the design argument, many theologians interpreted his research as reflecting the self-evolving powers of nature which they attributed to a Supreme Deity. Darwin himself, however, made no religious assertions in his research, keeping his observations focused solely on science and reason. Regarding human evolution, he simply wrote:

"As many more individuals of each species are born than can possibly survive; and as, consequently, there is a frequently recurring struggle for existence, it follows that any being, if it vary however slightly in any manner profitable to itself, under the complex and sometimes varying conditions of life, will have a better chance of surviving, and thus be naturally selected. From the strong principle of inheritance, any selected variety will tend to propagate its new and modified form."

— **Darwin, *"On the Origins of Species"*, 1858.**

Huxley admired the theories contained within Darwin's work as they marked a clear division between religion and science, a step he believed was crucial in an age where religion exerted a great deal of influence over scientific discoveries. It must be noted, however, that Darwin did not intend to deny the existence of God through his postulations, for though his religious faith crumbled after the death of his daughter, he avoided writing or speaking on the subject of religion in fear of causing pain to his loved ones – namely his wife who was a devoted Christian. Although Darwinism led to a resurgence of atheism in the modern world, it is interesting to consider that Darwin was generally known to identify himself primarily as an agnostic, rather than an atheist, when asked about his views on the existence of God.

Eminent philosopher and biologist of the Victorian era, Herbert Spencer (1820-1903), also made significant contributions in the arena of agnostic philosophy. He is accredited for coining the phrase *"survival of the fittest"* to illustrate the Darwinian concept of natural selection, extending it to sociological and political paradigms. As an ardent agnostic, Spencer took much of Darwin's discoveries to be a testament to the theory of human evolution. As for his stance on agnosticism, he claimed not to undermine religion in the face of science as Huxley did, but rather make peace between the two. In reference to the theory of evolution, he underlined the central idea in Darwin's discovery to be that of an Unknowable phenomenon which we strive to understand in, both, science and religion.

"Those who cavalierly reject the Theory of Evolution, as not adequately supported by facts, seem quite to forget that their own theory is supported by no facts at all. Like the majority of men who are born to a given belief, they demand the most rigorous proof of any adverse belief, but assume that their own needs none."

— **Spencer, *"The Development Hypothesis"*, 1852.**

Whether one perceives this Unknown phenomenon to be the Creator of the Universe, or the ultimate stage in illumination, Spencer concluded that religion and science must reconcile on the grounds that perceiving the totality of Absolute Reality is beyond the capacity of the human mind. The knowledge we have or seek regarding the Unknown in its absolute form, therefore, is only but "relative knowledge", and not the whole of it. According to him, the Unknown was the final stage in the process of evolution wherein Man would reach perfection, having passed through his initial existence as an indefinite, simple and incoherent being. The proposition soon came to be known as "Spencerism", taking after Darwin's theory of evolution to predict that ultimately only the strongest, most adaptable species would survive.

9

NON-RELIGION

There is some debate over the description of non-religion as an ideology distinct from atheism and agnosticism or simply an extension of similar anti-theistic sentiments. While it is true that often atheism and agnosticism are both colored in the shade of 'non-religion', it is important to understand that non-religion, itself, is most commonly defined as an absence of religion. It is generally entwined with the beliefs of atheists and agnostics simply because it can also refer to hostility or uncertainty towards religion – or even the complete rejection of the phenomenon. Although atheists and agnostics consider themselves fundamentally non-religious, it is worth noting that some people, who are neither atheists nor agnostics, exercise a complete indifference towards religion, and it is they who most aptly fit the description of being non-religious.

Perhaps the most distinguishing feature of non-religious ideology is that it does not set to prove or disprove religion or God's existence since neither proposition would cause them to change themselves or their lives, in the very least. This attitude is often the result of a deep contemplation regarding the nature of ethics and morality. In addition, it seeks to explore the following question: *Would* humanity choose to live by moral virtues in the absence of God or religion? As such, non-religion can be interpreted, in many cases, as a stark contrast to religious dogma wherein a specific religious ideology is imposed upon all, regardless of people's personal beliefs and values. In doing so, religion sets the standard of what is and is not desirable behavior, thereby dictating a specific way of life which, in some cases, might only benefit a select few or further the division between believers and non-believers.

The historical origins of non-religion can be vaguely traced to freethinkers of the 18th century, including Kant who popularized the concept of "indifferentism" in his *"Critique of Pure Reason"*. Deeply embedded in the theory of moral relativism, indifferentism proposed the equality of all religious faiths, advocating religious pluralism instead of a complete dismissal of religion altogether. This was to ensure that one religion does not attempt to dogmatize others or seek to overshadow the rest. Religious authorities, however, did not support the notion of advancing faiths other than their own, thus leading to a blatant inequality and discrimination on the basis of religion – as in the case of the Catholic Church during the Enlightenment era or the French Revolution.

Consequently, religion surfaced as a divisive force, rather than a potential instrument that could harmonize a diverse society. Some philosophers ultimately came to the conclusion that the basis of morality should not be confined to the tenets of religion, but rather be embraced as a human necessity or obligation, regardless of religious differences. Freethinkers the likes of Jean-Jacques Rousseau, for instance, supported non-religious sentiments after having witnessed the innumerable crimes perpetuated in the name of religion. Although initially a devoted Calvinist, he – despite his deteriorating religious convictions – redeemed his faith in deism, whereby he considered all of creation to contain a Divinity which he attributed to the ultimate Creator. In the 18th century, deism was deemed one of many types of non-religion. Despite its distinction from Catholicism and Calvinism, it led Rousseau to develop a strong inclination towards nature and redefine moral philosophy:

"The first man who, having fenced in a piece of land, said "This is mine," and found people naïve enough to believe him, that man was the true founder of civil society. From how many crimes, wars, and murders, from how many horrors and misfortunes might not any one have saved mankind, by pulling up the stakes, or filling up the ditch, and crying to his fellows: Beware of listening to this impostor; you are undone if you once forget that the fruits of the earth belong to us all, and the earth itself to nobody."

— Rousseau, *"Discourse on Inequality"*, 1754.

Although his views originally reflected, in large part, the core philosophy of indifferentism, going against many of the orthodox Catholic and Calvinist doctrines, he nevertheless played an important part in influencing moral philosophy and paved way for 19th century Romanticism. In the Age of Enlightenment, discussions on morality and ethics became less centered on religion and more focused on logic and reason, encouraging ideas of free-speech and liberalism. While some became more vocal about their anti-religious sentiments, others expressed non-religious beliefs through skepticism and humanism, reiterating that humanity did not necessarily need religion to maintain the code of morality.

Although secularism, as discussed in aforementioned pages, is largely associated with atheism, it is also a key indicator of non-religious ideology. There are many people who support humanist secularism, though they do not identify themselves as atheists. They simply advocate the idea of living in a society where the law is equal for all, regardless of religion. In this case, the basis of morality is defined by Humanism, which holds that the right actions are those that maximize pleasure and minimize suffering, and that belief in God or the supernatural is not imperative for moral behavior. As a non-religious school of thought, humanist secularism is intertwined with utilitarianism – an ideology that portrays pleasure or happiness as the ultimate motive for virtuous or noble action. This led to a new basis for moral discipline, made popular by Jeremy Bentham and John Stuart Mill, which was "hedonism", also known as classic utilitarianism. Their ideas, however, were strikingly similar to those of Hume, who wrote:

"In all determinations of morality, this circumstance of public utility is ever principally in view; and wherever disputes arise, either in philosophy or common life, concerning the bounds of duty, the question cannot, by any means, be decided with greater certainty, than by ascertaining, on any side, the true interests of mankind."

— Hume, *"An Enquiry Concerning the Nature of Morals"*, 1751.

In the modern world, humanism is most strongly tied to non-religion, since it does not seek to eliminate religion nor advance the ideology. Ideas of free-speech and free-thought are encouraged, and moral boundaries are drawn on the basis of sentiments, not reason.

10

CONCLUSION

While different faiths of the world vary from each other to a great degree, each ideology offers a fresh perspective about life and the nature of reality. Often, atheism and agnosticism may even seem to be at war with each other, while non-religion might appear to go against the very foundations of theism; yet advocates of these philosophies inadvertently contribute a great deal to each other, thus revealing a strong interconnectedness between them despite their many differences. It is through a profound, unbiased exploration of atheism, agnosticism and non-religion that the three ultimately manifest as a response to the same phenomenon or Reality that each of us seeks or struggles to fathom. Although we may respond to this Reality differently and choose a path that seems to go against another, in due course, our paths are inextricably tied in the search for purpose and meaning. Regardless of what path we take, it is important to remember that, despite our imperfections, we are all people of an equal existence, capable of giving and receiving Love – which is, in itself, a reality powerful enough to unite us.

Symbols of Agnosticism, Atheism and Non-Religion

Statement of Faith for the Universal Life Church Monastery of Massachusetts

God or your higher power is holy and calls us to be a holy people.

God or your higher power, who is holy, has abundant and steadfast love for us. God or your higher power 's holy love is revealed to us in the life and teachings, death and resurrection of Jesus Christ, our Savior and Lord. God or your higher power continues to work, giving life, hope and salvation through the indwelling of the Holy Spirit, drawing us into God or your higher powers own holy, loving life. God or your higher power transforms us, delivering us from sin, idolatry, bondage, and self-centeredness to love and serve God or your higher power, others, and to be stewards of creation. Thus, we are renewed in the image of God or your higher power as revealed in Jesus Christ.

Apart from God or your higher power, no one is holy. Holy people are set apart for God or your higher power 's purpose in the world. Empowered by the Holy Spirit, holy people live and love like Jesus Christ. Holiness is both gift and response, renewing and transforming, personal and communal, and ethical. The holy people of God or your higher power follow Jesus Christ in engaging all the cultures of the world and drawing all peoples to God or your higher power.

Holy people are not legalistic or judgmental. They do not pursue an exclusive, private state of being better than others. Holiness is not flawlessness but the fulfillment of God or your higher power 's intention for us. The pursuit of holiness can never cease because love can never be exhausted.

God or your higher power wants us to be, think, speak, and act in the world in a spiritual manner. We invite all to embrace God or your higher power 's call to:

- be filled with all the fullness of God or your higher power;
- live lives that are devout, pure, and reconciled, thereby being an agent of transformation in the world;
- live as a faithful covenant people, building accountable community, growing up, embodying the spirit of God or your higher power 's law in holy love;
- exercise for the common good an effective array of ministries and callings, according to the diversity of the gifts of the Holy Spirit;
- practice compassionate ministries, solidarity with the poor, advocacy for equality, justice, reconciliation, and peace; and
- care for the earth, God or your higher power 's gift in trust to us, working in faith, hope, and

confidence for the healing and care of all creation.

By the grace of God or your higher power, let us covenant together to be a holy people.

May this call impel us to rise to this vision of Spiritual mission:

• Preach the transforming message of spirtituality
• Teach the principles of love and forgiveness;
• Embody lives that reflect honesty and togetherness;
• Lead in engaging with the cultures of the world; and
• Partner with others to multiply its effect for the reconciliation of all things.

For this we live and labor to the glory of God or your higher power.

Formation of our ministry: the

Universal Life Church Monastery of Massachusetts

...ordination is a personal calling by God to minister others. I received my calling on several occasions. I didn't understand why at those times. The first was in May 1990. The second time was in May 1998- at this time, I was going through a difficult period in a marriage and prayed for guidance. In May 2004 is was finishing my studies to receive an MBA and felt like my life was not as full as it could be. This last time, in May 2010, I felt as though many people were always turning to me for advice and comfort and I felt at peace with myself and extremely happy. I am ready to spread my knowledge and his word to all that will listen. Please join me.

ABOUT THE AUTHOR

Oracle Claretta Pam was ordained by the Universal Life Church Monastery headquartered in Seattle, WA. Oracle Pam believes that ultimately we are all one. The path chosen to spirituality is available to all that seek it. She is an Interdenominational Oracle that performs ministerial functions and offers services that include: weddings, civil unions, baptisms, naming ceremonies, life coach services, private ministerial services, house blessings, hospital visitations and funerals. The Oracle is the author of several divinity books and a Guide to Divinity that covers more than 30 religions, belief systems and faiths.

JOURNAL

NOTES

JOURNAL

NOTES

JOURNAL

NOTES

JOURNAL

NOTES

JOURNAL

NOTES

JOURNAL

NOTES

JOURNAL

NOTES

JOURNAL

NOTES

JOURNAL

NOTES

JOURNAL___________________________________

NOTES___________________________________

JOURNAL

NOTES

JOURNAL

NOTES

JOURNAL

NOTES

JOURNAL

NOTES

JOURNAL

NOTES

JOURNAL

NOTES

JOURNAL

NOTES

JOURNAL

NOTES

JOURNAL

NOTES

JOURNAL

NOTES

JOURNAL

NOTES

JOURNAL

NOTES

JOURNAL

NOTES

JOURNAL

NOTES

JOURNAL

NOTES

JOURNAL

NOTES

JOURNAL

NOTES

JOURNAL

NOTES

JOURNAL

NOTES

JOURNAL

NOTES

JOURNAL

NOTES

JOURNAL

NOTES

JOURNAL

NOTES

JOURNAL

NOTES

JOURNAL

NOTES

JOURNAL

NOTES

JOURNAL

NOTES

JOURNAL

NOTES

JOURNAL

NOTES

JOURNAL

NOTES

JOURNAL

NOTES

JOURNAL

NOTES

JOURNAL

NOTES

JOURNAL____

NOTES____

JOURNAL

NOTES

JOURNAL

NOTES

JOURNAL

NOTES

JOURNAL

NOTES

JOURNAL

NOTES

JOURNAL

NOTES

JOURNAL

NOTES

JOURNAL

NOTES

JOURNAL

NOTES

JOURNAL

NOTES

JOURNAL

NOTES

JOURNAL

NOTES

JOURNAL

NOTES

JOURNAL

NOTES

JOURNAL

NOTES

JOURNAL

NOTES

JOURNAL

NOTES

JOURNAL

NOTES

JOURNAL

NOTES

JOURNAL

NOTES

JOURNAL

NOTES

JOURNAL

JOURNAL

JOURNAL

JOURNAL

JOURNAL

JOURNAL

JOURNAL

JOURNAL

JOURNAL

JOURNAL

JOURNAL

JOURNAL

JOURNAL

JOURNAL

JOURNAL

JOURNAL

JOURNAL

JOURNAL

JOURNAL

JOURNAL

JOURNAL

JOURNAL

JOURNAL

JOURNAL

JOURNAL

JOURNAL

JOURNAL

JOURNAL

JOURNAL

JOURNAL

JOURNAL

JOURNAL

JOURNAL

JOURNAL

JOURNAL

JOURNAL

JOURNAL

JOURNAL

JOURNAL

JOURNAL

JOURNAL

JOURNAL

JOURNAL____

JOURNAL

JOURNAL

JOURNAL

JOURNAL

JOURNAL

JOURNAL

JOURNAL

JOURNAL

JOURNAL

JOURNAL

JOURNAL

JOURNAL

JOURNAL

JOURNAL

JOURNAL

JOURNAL

JOURNAL

JOURNAL

JOURNAL

JOURNAL

JOURNAL

JOURNAL

JOURNAL

JOURNAL

JOURNAL

JOURNAL

JOURNAL

JOURNAL

JOURNAL

JOURNAL

JOURNAL

JOURNAL

JOURNAL

JOURNAL

JOURNAL

JOURNAL

JOURNAL

JOURNAL

JOURNAL

JOURNAL

JOURNAL

JOURNAL

Agnosticism, Atheism and Non-Religion

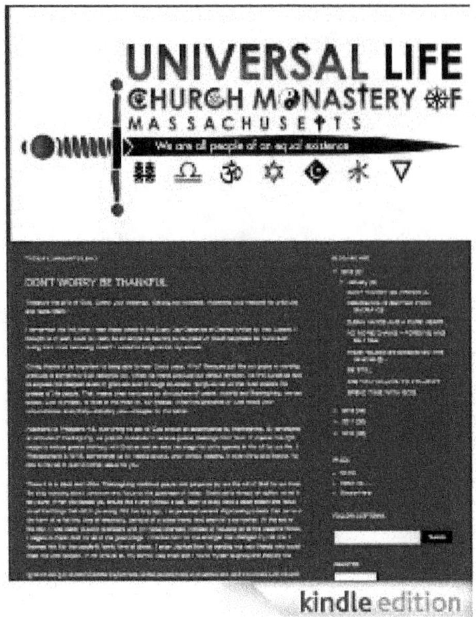
UNIVERSAL LIFE
CHURCH MONASTERY OF
MASSACHUSETTS
We are all people of an equal existence
kindle edition

FIND US ONLINE

https://twitter.com/ULCMM

https://www.facebook.com/ULCMM

http://ulcmm.blogspot.com/

http://ministers.themonastery.org/profile/OracleCPam

http://ulcmm.com

For membership inquiries please see us online at http://ulcmm.com

Agnosticism, Atheism and Non-Religion

Other forthcoming books available by Oracle Claretta Pam

Agnosticism Atheism Non-Religion
Bahai Faith
Buddhism
Cao Dai
Catholicism
Christianity
Confucianism
Hinduism
Humanism
Islam
Jainism
Jehovas Witnesses
Juche North Korea
Judaism
Natural Law
Neopaganism
New Age
Primal Faith
Primal Indigenous
Rastafarianism
Scientology
Shinto
Sikhism
Spiritism
Taoism
Tarahumara Beliefs
Tenrikyo
The Occult
African Traditional - Diasporic
Unificationism
Unitarian Universalism
Zoroastrianism

Innovative Publishers

SACREDVISION
PRESS

www.ingramcontent.com/pod-product-compliance
Lightning Source LLC
Chambersburg PA
CBHW060254100426
42742CB00011B/1747

* 9 7 8 1 4 9 1 3 1 6 2 0 7 *